RIDING THE RAILS

TRAINS THEN AND NOW

RIDING THE RAILS

TRAINS THEN AND NOW

Steve Otfinoski

BENCHMARK BOOKS

MARSHALL CAVENDISH
NEW YORK

Benchmark Books
Marshall Cavendish Corporation
99 White Plains Road
Tarrytown, New York 10591-9001

Library of Congress Cataloging-in-Publication Data
Otfinoski, Steven.
Riding the rails : trains then and now / by Steven Otfinoski.
    p.   cm. — (Here we go!)
Includes bibliographical references and index.
Summary: A simple introduction to railroads both past and present.
ISBN 0-7614-0404-X (lib. bdg.)
1. Railroads—Juvenile literature. [1. Railroads.] I.Title II.Series: Here we
go! (New York, N.Y.)
TF148.O74   1997   625.1—dc20   96-19160   CIP   AC

Photo research by Matthew Dudley

Cover photo: *Photo Researchers, Inc.*, David Weintraub

The photographs in this book are used by permission and through the
courtesy of: *The Image Bank:* L. Dennis, 1; Michael Skott, 2; Steve
Satushek, 6–7; Cliff Feulner, 10; Place, 11; Janeart LTD., 14; Alan Becker,
15; Garry Gay, 16; Michael Melford, 18; Don Landwehrle, 21; Pete Turner,
22, 26, 27; Co Rentmeester, 23; Stephen Wilkes, 28–29; Gary Crallé, 30;
Merrell Wood, 32. *Photo Researchers, Inc.:* Jerry Irwin, 15 (top); Peter
Skinner, 19; David R. Frazier, 20; I. J. Strange, 22–23; Japan Airlines, 27
(bottom); Jeff Smith (back cover). *Corbis-Bettmann:* 8, 12, 13 (top &
bottom). *The Granger Collection:* 8–9. *Arms Communications:*
Hans Halberstadt, 16–17; Howard Ande, 17; Brian Solomon, 24, 25.

Printed in the United States of America

6   5   4   3   2   1

To Beverly,

who hates the plane, but loves the train

RTHERN PACIFIC

Have you ever heard a train whistle
blow in the middle of the night?
Do you wonder where the train
is going or where it's coming from?
Would you like to hop on board
and take a ride on the rails?
Trains filled with people and goods
have been rumbling along America's
tracks for some two hundred years.

Trains are pulled by a locomotive.
Early locomotives were powered by steam.
In 1829, George Stephenson, an
Englishman, built a locomotive that carried
passengers on daily runs. He called it the
Rocket, but at top speed it only chugged
along at thirty-six miles per hour.

One year later in New York, Peter Cooper challenged
a horse–drawn train to a race with his steam
locomotive, Tom Thumb.
Tom Thumb was ahead in the race when an engine
belt slipped.
The train came to a dead stop. The horse won the race!
But it was the "iron horse" that would have the
last laugh.
The train was here to stay.

Wherever the railroad went, people went, too.
Towns and cities sprang up along train routes.
At the center of every town was a station.

The people who worked the rails
were proud of their trains.
They took good care of each car—
from the powerful locomotive to the
colorful caboose. The caboose was
where the workers ate and slept.

Workers laid track through mountains.
They felled trees, dug tunnels, and built wooden bridges called trestles.
As they worked, they sang songs like "I've Been Working on the Railroad."
They told stories about other railroad men who'd done incredible things.

One great train story is about an engineer named Casey Jones.
Casey always brought his train in on time.
When he found himself running late one day, he picked up speed.
He didn't see a freight train sitting on the track ahead.
until it was too late.
Casey slammed on the brakes and stayed at his post.
He died in the wreck, but all the passengers lived.
Casey Jones, the brave engineer, remains a folk hero to this day.

By the early twentieth century, railroads took people just about anywhere. Trains hugged mountainsides, plowed through winter snows, and raced across plains and ranches. Locomotives had cattle guards on the front to push away cows or other animals that might stray onto the rails.

By the 1950s, diesel trains were replacing steam
locomotives.
Their engines burned fuel cleaner, and they could
go faster, too.
Train lines like the Union Pacific and the Santa Fe
were famous for getting to their destinations
on time.

Today, trains carry more freight and fewer passengers.
Freight cars come in all shapes and sizes.
These hopper cars (above) are carrying coal.
The coal is emptied out through chutes in the bottom
of the cars.
The tanker cars (right) are carrying liquid cargo.
There are also boxcars, flatcars, and refrigerator cars.

Where do trains go when they're not moving?
Freight cars (left) sit in a huge freight yard until they're needed.
These commuter trains are resting on side rails at the station.
They take passengers to New York City for work or fun and then back home to the suburbs at night.

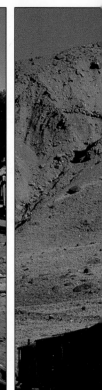

Trains carry people and freight to every corner
of the world.
A diesel grinds to a halt in a small Egyptian town.
Another winds through the Andes in Argentina.
Passengers are carrying their baggage, ready to climb
on board a train in Africa's Ivory Coast.
It might be hard to find a seat!

Some trains run on electricity supplied by overhead wires,
like this commuter train in Montreal.
Trolley cars are a cross between a train and a bus.
They are electric, too, and run along tracks in city streets.
This one climbs up and down San Francisco's
steep hills at a steady pace.

Many new trains look very different from the older
models of electric or diesel trains.

The Japanese bullet train (above) lives up to its name.
It can travel over 125 miles per hour.

The French TGV (top right) has been clocked at
300 miles per hour when it had no passengers in it.

The Japanese magnetic train (bottom right) needs
no locomotive and no fuel. Magnets make it move.
It floats above the ground on a magnetic field.

Trains have come a long way since George Stephenson's Rocket.
If all the tracks on earth were set end to end they would reach to the moon and back again—eight times!
There's nothing quite like a ride on the rails.

FIND OUT MORE

Barton, Byron. *Trains.* New York: HarperCollins, 1986.

Broekel, Ray. *Trains.* Chicago: Childrens Press, 1981.

Gibbons, Gail. *Trains.* New York: Holiday House, 1987.

Rockwell, Anne. *Trains.* New York: Puffin Books, 1994.

Usborne, Peter. *Trains.* New York: Grosset & Dunlap, 1971.

Wood, Sydney. *Trains & Railroads.* New York: Dorling Kindersley, 1992.

INDEX

STEVE OTFINOSKI has written more than sixty books for children. He also has a theater company called *History Alive!* that performs plays for schools about people and events from the past. Steve lives in Stratford, Connecticut, with his wife and two children.